MW00534853

Isabel McNeill Carley Orff Essentials Collection

Recorder Improvisation and Technique

BOOK ONE

Beginning with the Soprano Recorder

Isabel McNeill Carley

Fourth Edition
Teacher and Student

Copyright © 2011-2023
Fourth Printing
Brasstown Press

B P

Brasstown Press
Charlottesville, VA
brasstownpress.com

Printed in USA
ISBN 978-0-9836545-0-6

Reviews of this Edition

"A unique approach to developing recorder technique through improvisation."

"A step-by-step process introduces basic recorder skills in a highly interactive context of singing, moving, responding to Kodaly hand signs, echo play, and accompanying on pitched and non-pitched percussion."

"Improvisation is a key component of the instruction; Carley's suggested exercises – presented in clear, incremental steps – make this model accessible for teachers regardless of previous experience."

> ~ **Leslie Timmons** in *American Recorder*

o

"The ideas for improvisation are varied and realistic for classroom use."

"Every lesson provides ideas and suggestions for integrating recorder with other media: singing, playing pitched and non-pitched instruments (ostinati). There is a flexibility around literacy which will provide a freedom for both teachers and students to follow the maxim of Carl Orff – 'Experience precedes cognition,' and which allows for the possibility of lots of real and rich music making opportunities from the very first class."

> ~ **Kim Kendrick** in *Ostinato*

o

Comments on previous editions of Recorder Improvisation and Technique

"Your recorder books are excellent ... completely in the spirit of the Schulwerk."

> ~ **Gunild Keetman**, co-creator with Carl Orff of the Orff Schulwerk

o

"The tunes are lovely, and even the patterns are satisfying."

> ~ **Miriam Samuelson**, founding member of the American Orff-Schulwerk Association

o

"Isabel Carley has given us a guide to musicianship. The recorder is only the means."

> ~ **Elizabeth Nichols**, founding member of the American Orff-Schulwerk Association

Acknowledgments

Hew Down the Tree from "The Dett Collection of Negro Spirituals Fourth Group (Auditorium Series Number 16)." Used with permission of the Publisher, Schmitt, Hall and McCreary Company Minneapolis, Minnesota.

Shady Grove and *Nottamun Town* from "Songs of All Time," Cooperative Recreation Service, Delaware, Ohio, 1957. Used with permission.

Taiwanese and Chinese folk songs, *Cross-Legged Woman, Lanterns Light, A Riddle, Three Cats, The Fisherman's Song, Rowing to Grandmother's House, The Bamboo Flute, Lullaby, The Train, Flowers in June, Frogs Jumping, Hard Work for a Grain of Rice, Longing for the Spring Breeze, The High Mountain, Heavy Rain, Harvest Festival, The Farm Village, Hare Hunting,* and *The Red-Cheeked Maiden* from "Songs Around the World," Sin-Lau Children's Music Center, Tainan, Taiwan, 1985. Used with permission.

o

Edited and produced by Brasstown Press with production assistance from Ayla Palermo.

Redesign of cover and symbols by Browning Porter Design, Charlottesville, VA.

o

Note on the fourth edition

This newly designed and reset edition of **Recorder Improvisation and Technique Book One** retains the contents of the third edition with the addition of expanded reference and resource materials.

CONTENTS

PART I ~ C PENTATONIC

CONTENTS continued

Care of Your Recorder

- Keep it in a cool dry place. Do not leave it outdoors, or in a vehicle in the sun, by a sunny window, or near a radiator. Wrap it in its case before you take it outside in cold weather. Blow gently into the instrument, covering the window in the mouthpiece with your finger, before you start to play.

- Always twist the joint in the same direction, whether putting the instrument together or taking it apart. Take it apart to dry after each playing.

- Your left hand goes on top, with your thumb covering the thumb-hole. Your right thumb supports the weight of the instrument, behind holes four and five (counting downward from the top). See also the recorder diagram at the beginning of Lesson 1.

- Lean the recorder on your lower lip and close your mouth over it.
  Never touch it with your teeth.

- Break in a new wooden recorder very gradually, playing only ten to fifteen minutes a day for the first two weeks to avoid permanent damage.

- Oil the inside of the bore of a wooden recorder every month with a light woodwind oil.

- Use cork grease on corked joints to make them air-tight and easy to adjust.

- If you are sharp (sounding too high-pitched) compared with your neighbor, try blowing more softly; or if needed, open the top joint slightly.

- Cover the holes with the pads of your fingers, not with the fingertips.

- Blow gently, beginning each tone with a "d" tonguing, and ending with a silent "t."

Instrument Abbreviations

Body Percussion

SN	Finger Snap	
CL	Clap	
P	Patsch (pat thigh)	**P L** = Left thigh; **P R** = Right thigh
ST	Stamp	

Recorder

SR	Soprano Recorder

Percussion

HD	Hand Drum
Dr	Drum
Sm Dr	Small Drum (Lesson 10)
FC	Finger Cymbals
TB	Temple Bell (Lesson 10)
Ti	Timpani
Cym	Cymbal(s)
Tr	Triangle
Tam	Tambourine
WB	Woodblock

Pitched Percussion (Orff Instruments)

SG	Soprano Glockenspiel
AG	Alto Glockenspiel
SX	Soprano Xylophone
AX	Alto Xylophone
BX	Bass Xylophone
AM	Alto Metallophone
BM	Bass Metallophone

Stringed Instruments

Gtr	Guitar (Lesson 10)
Bs	Bass (optional, instead of **BX**)

Three Gapped Pentatonic Scales with Hand Signs

Name	Hand sign	C Pentatonic (RIT One Part I)	G Pentatonic (RIT One Part II)	F Pentatonic (RIT One Part III)
Do'	[eye level]	C'	G'	F'
[Ti]				
La		A	E'	D'
So		G	D'	C'
[Fa]				
Mi		E	B	A
Re		D	A	G
Do	[waist height]	C	G	F

In this and all **RIT** books, *Do* is moveable. For example, the same hand sign for *Do* refers to **C** (in Part I), **G** (in Part II), and **F** (in Part III).

See *About Pentatonic Scales and Modes*, pp. 62-63, for more illustrations and applications.

Carley ○ Recorder Improvisation and Technique Book One ○ Fourth Edition

Reading, Writing, and Saying Rests and Time Names

Notes	Stick Notes	Rests	Time Names
♩		≹	*Taa*
♫	⊓	ˀ	*Ta-tee*
♩		▬	*Taa-aa*
♩.		▬ ≹	*Taa-aa-aa*
𝅝		▬	*Taa-aa-aa-aa*
3 ♫♪	⊓⊓	≹ ˀ	*Ta-te-tee*

Tags

Tags are pointers used throughout the Lessons, as follows:

Echo	Repeat exactly what you hear.
Focus	Pay close attention.
Improvise	Invent new music, solo and with others.
Q+A	Improvise complementary phrases - the *Question* remains musically and/or rhythmically open, ready for a more final-sounding *Answer*.

Guidelines

- For visual simplicity, voice and soprano recorder (SR) parts are notated as unison, although SR actually sounds one octave higher.

- Suggested instrumentation appears throughout the Lessons. Substitutions are of course permissible where necessary.

- A fermata over a note in an ostinato pattern suggests where to end a short coda when the rest of the ensemble has stopped. See, for example, p. 38 (glockenspiel) and p. 53 (Step 4 ⑧).

Introduction

This book, concisely known as **RIT One**, is a superb beginner's primer and foundational guide to playing the soprano recorder. Eleven tightly integrated lessons introduce the student to the recorder repertoire and technique in short exercises that partner the teacher with the student. The emphasis is not simply on rote learning, but on a collaborative process that develops musical and technical skills by actually making music. From the beginning, there are songs for the student to play, improvisations to nurture the musical imagination, and ensemble materials to deliver the excitement of rhythmic layering and patterning.

Suitable for the classroom or private instruction, the carefully designed framework of interactions between the teacher and student has proved successful with children, teens, and adults. Each lesson features improvised and collaboratively composed exercises, making the learning process dynamic and spontaneous, without regimentation. The pace can be swift, too, so that students who respond well to challenging instruction will be particularly engaged.

With **RIT One**, newcomers to the soprano recorder learn more than simple major tonalities as they become acquainted with gapped pentatonic scales, including minor modes. Each lesson builds on the last, introducing new notes, new concepts, and a diverse repertoire of vocal and instrumental arrangements–including Orff instruments and body percussion.

Divided in three parts, the book now features an expanded Table of Contents listing all the major topics, instruments used, and repertoire. Part I (Lessons 1-7) introduces C pentatonic scales and sounds. Then Part II (Lessons 8-9) moves to music in G pentatonic, with additional ear-training opportunities. Finally, Part III (Lessons 10-11) brings materials in F pentatonic modes to complete the beginning course. By the end of **RIT One**, the student will have played all the notes from low C to high G.

By design, vivid musical experiences start at once. Throughout the lessons, echo-play, improvised phrases, and Kodaly hand-sign and sight-reading practice help ease awkward fingering transitions, and encourage technical proficiency. Other exercises demonstrate how to combine musical elements into new songs with layered ostinati. Using only a few notes in the first lessons, but always enlivened by colorations like syncopation, rhythmic drive, counterpoint, and new time signatures, the student musicians gain immediate satisfaction as everyone joins the ensemble.

Even the youngest participants, or those with little musical training, naturally become self-assured as their own invented music becomes part of a larger piece shared with the group. **RIT One** lives up to its aim: Put improvisation before technique in a learning strategy that combines recorders, voice, and body percussion with Orff ensemble and other instruments. The resulting music is delightfully new each time, the short-term result of this creative process. Repeat, often, and along with technical skill and confidence in playing the recorder, a deeper musical understanding will be the happy long-term outcome for students and teachers alike.

Brasstown Press

PART I ~ C PENTATONIC

Lesson 1

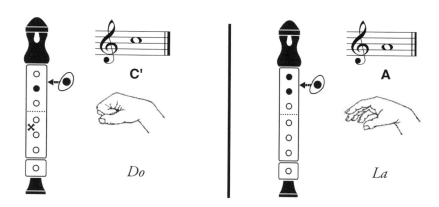

Pick up your recorder. Your LEFT thumb covers the hole on the back. The first three fingers of your LEFT hand will rest near the first three holes below the mouthpiece.

Place your RIGHT thumb on the back, opposite and between the fourth and fifth holes, to support the instrument. Your RIGHT fingers will be in position, ready to cover the four lower holes, as you learn the notes.

1. Follow Teacher's hand signs and play long notes as Teacher indicates. Listen that each tone begins with "d" and ends with a silent "t"; listen that each tone starts, stays, and ends at the same pitch. (See **Three Gapped Pentatonic Scales with Hand Signs**, page iii.)

2. Say, "Taa" for ♩ = 1 beat; "Taa-a" for ♩ = 2 beats; "Ta-tee" for ♫ = 2 half beats; "Taa-aa-aa-aa" for 𝅝 = 4 beats. (See **Reading, Writing, and Saying Rests and Time Names**, page iv.)

3. **Echo** Copy exactly what you hear Teacher play, using only the two notes **C′** and **A**. Sing "*Do*" and "*La*" and finger the pattern on your recorder before you play each pattern, *e.g.*:

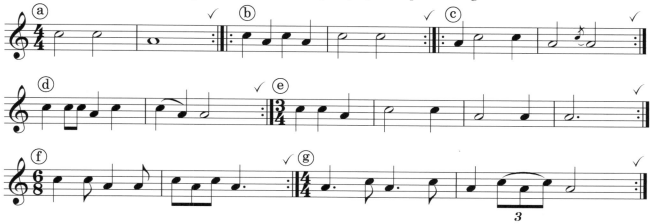

4. **Improvise** Take turns being Teacher, making up **C′- A** phrases for the class or your practice partner to echo.

5. Practice making up and echoing your own phrases.

   Focus Make up a whole echo piece to play for the class by heart.

6. **Improvise** Play "Pass it on" around the class in pairs. Number one in each pair makes up a **C′- A** phrase for number two to echo. Then reverse, with all number twos making up the phrase, all number ones echoing.

Goin' down to Cairo

Illinois
arr. Isabel Carley

Cairo sounds like "KAY-row," rhymes with "play-show."

PATTERNS - GOIN' DOWN TO CAIRO

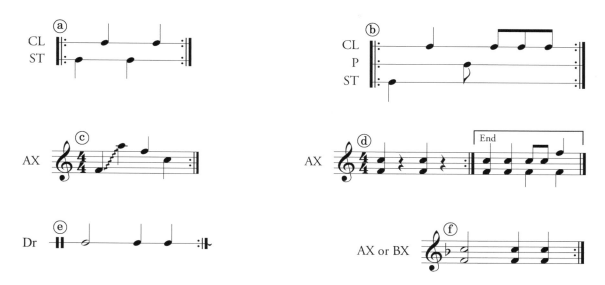

1. Try different ways of doing **Goin' down to Cairo**, using voices and recorders, solos and choruses, rhythm patterns, rhythm instruments, *etc.* (See **Instrument Abbreviations**, page ii.)

2. Play the tune on a glockenspiel, using mallets in both hands.

   You will need **C D F G A B♭** and **C'**. Remove **E** and replace **B** with **B♭**.

March

Isabel Carley

1. **Echo** Fill in the empty bars, echoing the first two bars:

Hew Down the Tree

United States

2. Wicked man is like the tree,

   Great shall his destruction be.

1. Sing **Hew Down the Tree** over Pattern ⓐ or ⓑ until you know it by heart.

2. Divide the class in half, with one group playing the recorder while the other half sings and does Pattern ⓐ, ⓑ, or ⓓ.

PATTERNS - HEW DOWN THE TREE

3. Add bar instruments on [**A** and **E**] or [**A C D E**] or **G**.

4. Repeat, reversing assignments.

READING

1. **Focus** Play what you see:

    Say "Taa-aa-aa" for 𝅗𝅥. = 3 beats; "Taa-aa-aa-aa" for 𝅝 = 4 beats; 𝄽 is a ♩ rest (a silent beat).

    Practice five times a day.

2. Add AX patterns on [**G** and **C**] or [**E** and **A**] to these tunes.

Lesson 2

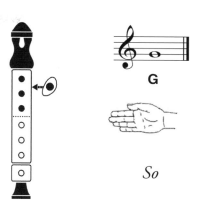

G

So

1. There are four basic tonguing techniques on the recorder:

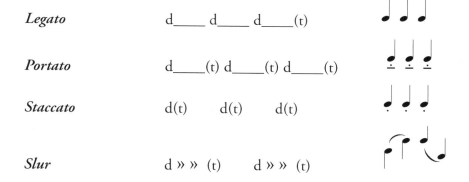

Legato	d____ d____ d____(t)
Portato	d____(t) d____(t) d____(t)
Staccato	d(t) d(t) d(t)
Slur	d » » (t) d » » (t)

Focus Follow Teacher's hand signs and play what Teacher's gestures suggest.

2. **Echo** Play exactly what Teacher plays, on **C′** and **A**; on **A** and **G**; on all three notes. Listen for Teacher's tonguing and play *exactly* what you hear:

    •   all together

    •   one at a time.

3. **Improvise** Take turns being Teacher, using two kinds of tonguing in each phrase you make up.

4. **Focus** Make up a **C' A G** piece and play it for the class by heart. Write it down so you can remember it, using stick notes and note names, or standard notation:

READING

1. **Focus** Play what you see. Clap and say time names / note names if you need to. What is another way of writing the time signature here?

How many different ways can you combine two of these short pieces into a longer piece?

E.g., ⓑ ⓑ ⓐ ⓑ ; ⓒ ⓓ ⓓ ⓒ ; ⓓ ⓐ ⓓ ⓐ ; *etc.*

2. **Focus** Play at sight. Repeat each exercise as needed, using *legato*, *staccato*, *portato*, or *slurs*. Practice very slowly; sedately; playfully; very fast.

3. Work out patterns using patsch and clap body percussion to fit your favorite two-piece combination of ⓐ - ⓓ above, and play it with a friend.

Cross-Legged Woman

Traditional Taiwanese Rhyme
Music by children of
St. Raphael Opportunity Center, Tainan

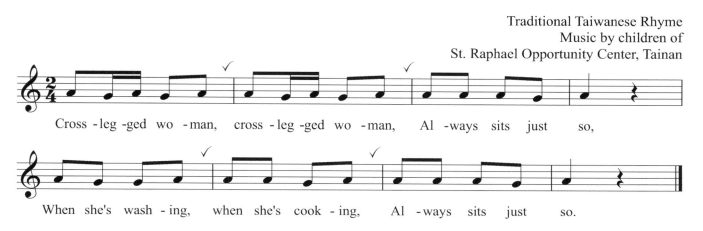

Cross -leg-ged wo -man, cross -leg-ged wo -man, Al -ways sits just so,

When she's wash -ing, when she's cook -ing, Al -ways sits just so.

PATTERNS

1. **Improvise** Make up answers to the following rhythm questions

   • all together

   • solo.

   There is space below for some of your answers.

   Q + A

2. **Q + A** Make up your own Questions to fit this Answer:

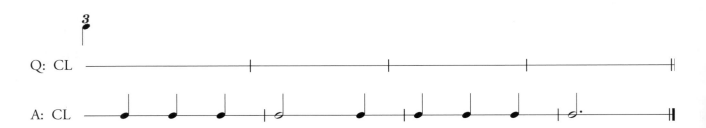

3. Make up a tune to fit the Question in Step 1, using only **C'**, **A** and **G**, singing with hand signs. Choose a tune from the class for the Question, and take turns making up an Answer

    • singing

    • playing.

4. Focus Make up a tune for the Answer in Step 2, singing with hand signs.

    Choose one for the whole class to play, and then take turns asking your own questions.

    Which were the best questions? Why?

5. Lead the class with hand signs in an improvised Question, using either the Answer tune from Step 4, or a new one of your own.

6. Q + A Play "Question and Answer" using **C' A G**:

Go around the class asking the same Question until you get tired of it. Then make up another.

7. Make up a Question and Answer with your practice partner, using all the notes you know.

8. Again, by yourself, with **A** as the final.

9. What makes a good Question? A good Answer?

10. Find two songs you know that have Q+A phrases in them. (The words need not be Q+A, just the tune.)

11. Play an *Ostinato* (a stubborn, repeated pattern) on **G** while Teacher improvises against it. Try these patterns for ostinati:

12. Transfer ⓐ, ⓑ, ⓒ, or ⓓ, to a body percussion ostinato, and take turns improvising over it on recorder.

Lesson 3

1. **Echo** Play what you hear Teacher play on **C′** and **A**; **A** and **G**; all three. *Listen for the tonguing.*

2. Take turns being Teacher, while the whole class echoes your SR or follows your hand signs.

3. Play Echo all around the class in pairs: Number one improvises a phrase for number two to echo. Again, with opposite assignments, without losing the beat.

4. **Focus** Play what you see:

   • Clap and say time names.

   • Say note names in rhythm and finger silently.

   • Play the tune, remembering to use legato tonguing unless it's marked otherwise.

   • Practice as needed, at various tempi.

5. Work out ostinati for ©️ and ⓓ using two kinds of body percussion. Then transfer them to rhythm instruments, *e.g.*, from Clap and Patsch to Cymbal and Drum:

6. **Focus** Over AX ostinato, play "Pass-it-on" all around the class, using only **C′ A** and **G**.

Did you come in on time? Was your phrase the same length as your neighbor's?

What is the tonal center?

7. **Echo** Play your own improvised phrases in **2/4**, **3/4**, **4/4** and **6/8** meter, using the notes **C′ A G** only.

Use these rhythm patterns as a basis if you wish:

8. **Q + A** Practice improvising your own Question+Answer phrases with the tonal center on: **C′**; on **A**; on **G**.
   What makes a good question? What makes a good answer?

9. Practice improvising with your practice partner, taking turns making up an ostinato on AX or a rhythm instrument, and improvising a tune. You can always repeat notes. Don't let yourself stop in the middle of a phrase. *Always start the ostinato first.*

10. **Improvise** Work out a longer piece using both Echo and Q+A phrases. Write it down if you wish in the space below, with stick notes and note names, or standard notation.

1. **Improvise** Make up echo phrases on **C' A G**. Take turns being Teacher.

2. Practice **Parade** silently while Teacher plays it. Clap the rhythm before you play.
   Echo one bar at a time until A is memorized.

3. Learn the HD (Hand Drum) part first with body percussion: ♩ = stamp; ♩ = clap.
   Then transfer the part to the drum.

4. **Focus** In the B section, the percussion part changes to WB (Woodblock).
   ⅞ is an ♪ (eighth-note) rest.

Parade

Isabel Carley

Lesson 4

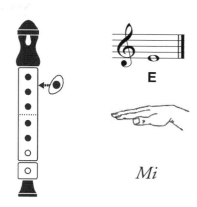

Mi

1. Finger silently the notes Teacher calls out as fast as you can, using **C' A G** and our new note, **E**.

2. **Echo** Play what you hear on **C** and **A**; on **G** and **E**; on **A G E**; on **C' A G E**. Take turns being Teacher in class.

    Focus Practice echoing your own **C' A G E** phrases at different tempi using each note in turn as the tonal center.

3. Go back and play through Lessons 1 and 2 on **G** and **E** instead of **C'** and **A**.

4. Follow Teacher's (or practice partner's) hand signs, and play what you see.

C'	*Do (D)*	
A	*La (L)*	
G	*So (S)*	
E	*Mi (M)*	

5. Play what you see. (The notes followed by "__" last twice as long):

    ⓐ *So La So Mi So La Do'__*‖   ⓑ *Mi So So__ Mi La La__*‖

    ⓒ *D' L L D' L S M__*‖   ⓓ *S L S L D__ D'__*‖

    Make up a tune putting two or three patterns from Step 5 together, like this: ⓑ ⓒ ⓑ ⓓ.

    Yours:_____

7. **Improvise** Make up two ideas of your own, ⓐ and ⓑ, using **C′ A G** and **E**, and see how many different ways you can combine them. *E.g.,* ⓐ ⓑ ⓐ ⓑ; ⓐ ⓑ ⓑ ⓐ; ⓐ ⓐ ⓑ ⓑ; *etc.*

   Yours:

   • _____

   • _____

8. **Focus** Play what you see. Practice as needed.

9. How many *different* ways can you play each pattern? Try staccato; legato; slurring in pairs; non-legato; and various combinations, *e.g.*:

10. Play one of these rhythms on **E** as an ostinato while Teacher improvises a tune over it:

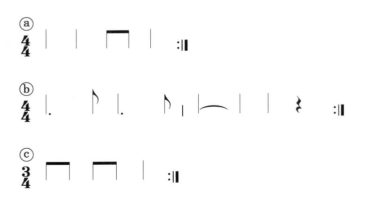

11. Take turns with your practice partner playing an ostinato on **E** and making up a tune.

IMPROVISATION

1. **Echo** Using **C′ A G E**, practice echoing your own phrases, using at least two kinds of tonguing in each phrase.

2. Improvise an echo piece, using phrases of different lengths, for variety.
   E.g. 4 bars :‖   2 bars :‖   4 bars :‖   1 bar :‖   Again, over an ostinato.

3. Work out and write down your own tune and setting for *Jellicle Cats.*

> Jellicle cats come out tonight,
> Jellicle cats come one, come all,
> The jellicle moon is shining bright,
> Jellicles come to the jellicle ball.
> ~ T. S. Eliot

   Include music for dancing at the ball if you wish.

4. **Improvise** Practice improvising Q+A phrases using all the notes you know (**C′ A G E**) over a drone on AX or BX

   - with **C** as the tonal center
   - with **A** as the tonal center
   - with **E** as the tonal center
   - with **G** as the tonal center.

5. Repeat your Question with a new Answer.

6. Repeat both Question and Answer.

Lanterns Light

Isabel Carley

Taiwan

1. Lan terns light,   Lan-terns bright,   shin - ing a - far on a moon-lit night.
2. Lan terns light,   Lan-terns bright,   cros - sing the bridge on a star - ry night.
3. Lan terns light,   Lan-terns bright,   twinkling in the river on a win - ter night.

The cymbal may be used in the rests.

Practice   •   clapping and saying time names.
Scherzo   •   saying note names and fingering silently.
                  •   singing and fingering.
                  •   playing as written.

Scherzo

Isabel Carley

PATTERNS

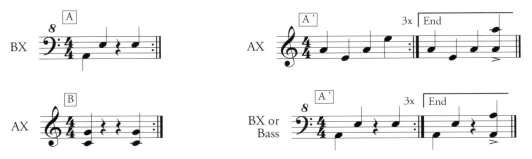

Lesson 5

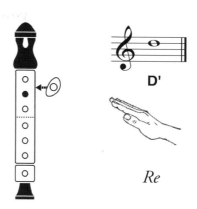

Re

1. **Echo** Play on **C′ A G** ; **A G E** ; **C′ A G E**, all around the class, taking turns making up a phrase and echoing your neighbor's phrase.
Again, reversing roles.

2. Practice silently shifting from **C′** to **D′**. Which finger moves? Be sure your RIGHT thumb supports the instrument securely, with your RIGHT forefinger holding lightly between finger holes 4 and 5.

3. **Focus** Play what you see. Repeat as needed.

4. **Q + A** Play Q+A using all the notes you know
   - with a partner
   - all around the class
   - by yourself.

   Decide first which note will be the tonal center. Where should your Question end?

5. **Focus** Work out a four-phrase piece with **D′** as the tonal center, using the form of a simple folk song. Be ready to play it by heart.

   E.g. **C′ A G C** ; **A G A E** ; **G E D E D E G__** ;
   C′ D′ C′ A ; **D E D E** ; **D G D A** ; **D A D′ A** , *etc.*

6. Low **D** is fingered as in the diagram. Almost
    all your fingers are covering holes.
    Finger the notes Teacher calls out, as fast as
    you can. (If your fingers move fast enough
    and precisely enough you can hear the pitch of
    each note as you go.)

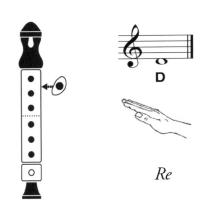

Re

7. ███ **Focus** ███ Play what you see. Repeat as needed.

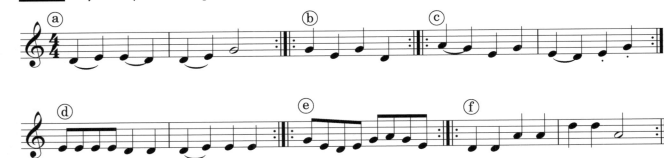

8. ███ **Focus** ███ Play **Parade** (Lesson 3) by heart on **C′ A G**. Then play it starting on **G**. What other notes will
    you need? ___ ___ Work out an accompaniment using AX and triangle for each version. Can you put
    them together in a longer form? What notes should AX play when the tune ends on **C′**? ___ ___
    On **G**? ___ ___

9. ███ **Q+A** ███ Play Q+A using **D E G A C′ D′** in *3/4* meter over AX or BX ostinato with:

Tonic	*Dominant*
C	**G**
A	**E**
G	**D**
D	**A**

Your Patterns should use only tonic and dominant, *E.g.:*

Rondo

Isabel Carley

1. **Focus** What is the form, if you use only **A** and **B**?
   What is the form, if you use **A** **B** and **C**?

2. What is the tonal center of **A**? ____
   What is the tonal center of **B**? ____
   What is the tonal center of **C**? ____
   What is the tonal center of **D**? ____

3. Work out an accompaniment for **A** using AX and finger cymbals. What notes should AX play?
   (Remove F and B bars first.)

4. Work out an accompaniment for **B** using two timps (or BX) and A G.

5. **Improvise** Work out patterns to fit **C** and **D**, using whatever instruments you choose.

6. Work out a circle dance for **A**; solos or duets for **B**, **C**, and **D** and put the Rondo together.

THREE FOLK SONGS

1. Echo Play exactly what your neighbor plays, on **D E G** ; **E G A** ; **D E G A**, one after another, all around the class. Then practice by yourself.

2. Q+A Make up Questions and Answers, on **D E G A** in a quick **2/4** meter, in slow **3/4** meter with **E** as the tonal center; in moderate **4/4** meter with **G** as the tonal center.

A Riddle

Taiwan

What can they be?   What can they be?   So close to-ge -ther but_ they'll ne -ver meet?

(Answers: ears; eyes; what else?)

PATTERNS

3. Echo clap in **4/4** meter using syncopated patterns like:

4. Echo over a rhythm ostinato. Use these patterns or your own.

Come Up, Horsey

United States

Come up,   hor -   sey   Hey,   hey,   Come up,   hor -   sey,

Hey,   hey,___   Come up,   hor -   sey,   Hey,   hey,

Come   up   hor -   sey,   Hey,   hey.

Three Cats

China

5. **Improvise** Make up three or more layered ostinati for this song. Use a combination of body percussion, drum, and Orff instruments.

6. Notice that the melody for **Three Cats** has measures of eighth notes and measures of half notes. If your ostinati provide more rhythmic interest in the measures where the melody has less, what will happen? See Steps 3 and 4 above for some ideas.

Lesson 6

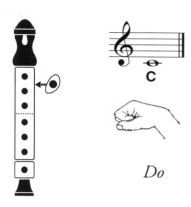

C

Do

1. Practice playing long notes softly on low **C**, starting each tone with a gentle "h" tonguing. Be sure your RIGHT hand fourth finger overreaches its hole enough to allow your fifth finger to cover its double hole completely. If your recorder has an adjustable bottom joint, turn it so it is comfortable for your hand.

2. |Focus| Play what you see:

Fais Dodo (Lullaby)

France

3. |Improvise| Make up your own Answer to the following Question.

Complete this!

Repeat the Question and give a more final Answer.

4. Choose two instruments to provide an ostinato accompaniment to Step 3 above.

5. Use 2 ⓓ as an ostinato while Teacher improvises a tune above it. Take turns being Teacher.

6. Practice the following exercises at various tempi, with as much variety of tonguing as possible
   (see Lesson 2 for a review if needed):

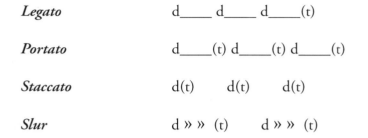

Legato	d_____ d_____ d_____(t)
Portato	d_____(t) d_____(t) d_____(t)
Staccato	d(t) d(t) d(t)
Slur	d » » (t) d » » (t)

Use combinations of the above four articulation techniques in the examples below.

7. Be careful to observe the articulation in the next three songs. Where nothing else is marked, use one of these tongued legato techniques, whichever works out best:

dah— dah— dah— *etc.*

d_th, d_th, *etc.*

The Fisherman's Song

Taiwan

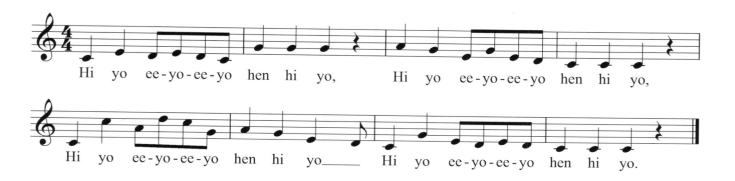

Hi yo ee-yo-ee-yo hen hi yo, Hi yo ee-yo-ee-yo hen hi yo,

Hi yo ee-yo-ee-yo hen hi yo____ Hi yo ee-yo-ee-yo hen hi yo.

Rowing to Grandmother's House

Isabel Carley

Taiwan

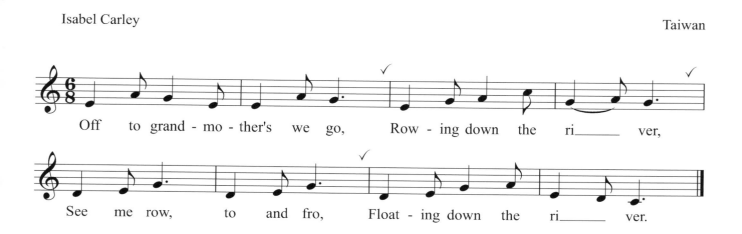

Off to grand-mo-ther's we go, Row-ing down the ri____ver,

See me row, to and fro, Float-ing down the ri____ver.

8. **Focus** Play **Shady Grove** at sight.

9. Practice until you know it by heart.

Shady Grove

Kentucky

Fanfare for Recorder and Drum

Isabel Carley

The Bamboo Flute

Isabel Carley   China

From the pur - ple bam - boo____ shoot,

For my child I'll make a flute.____

Hold your flute just so Then be - gin to blow,

From your flute will come love - ly me - lo - dies.

Try it a - gain: [Whistle]____ Now you play.

Try once a - gain: [Whistle]____ Now you

play.____ [Whistle]____

Lesson 7

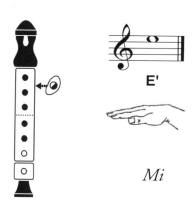

Mi

1. **Focus** High **E′** is fingered just like low **E**, except that the thumb hole must be partly opened. Try it starting with low **E** and rocking your LEFT wrist up and out until a crack opens at the thumb hole and a stronger "d" tonguing produces high **E′**.

2. Work out an ostinato using only **E** octaves over which Teacher improvises, with **A** as the tonal center. Take turns being Teacher. *E.g.*:

3. **Improvise** Add a simple drone on AX or BX on [**A** - **E**], and try it again, using volunteers on solos to make this form (change the ostinato in **B** if you wish):

   [A] [A]¹   Q+A : Q+A¹
   [B]   Echo : Echo
   [A]¹   Q+A¹

4. Play what you see:
   • silently
   • slowly.
   Practice as needed with various tonguings:

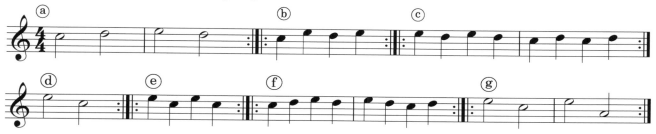

5. **Echo** Make up echo phrases using high **E′ D′ C′** ; **A C′ D′ E′** ; **G A C′ D′ E′**.
   Use different meters and different tonal centers

   - in class
   - with a partner
   - by yourself.

6. Using all the notes you know, improvise a dance in **6/8** meter in this form:

A	Q + A′	with **C** as the tonal center
B	Echo : Echo	with **G** as the tonal center
A	Q + A	with **C** as the tonal center

   Choose a different bar instrument to accompany each section.
   Be sure the accompaniment pattern starts first.

7. **Focus** Do the same assignment in Step 6 by yourself with **D** as the tonal center of **A** and **C** as the
   tonal center of **B**. Keep it simple so you can remember your Question.
   If you find one you want to remember, write it down and work out patterns to go with it.

8. What other forms could you make using only two musical ideas?

Lullaby

Taiwan

Shoes of Deerskin

Ojibway

PATTERNS

This is a follow-the-leader game. The players must watch the movement of the leader to know how fast, how loud, how smoothly, how perkily to play. These patterns are simply a few possibilities. Don't try to use them all at once! Make up others of your own.

The Train

Taiwan

What is the tonal center? _____

Flowers in June

Taiwan

What is the tonal center? _____

PART II ~ G PENTATONIC

Lesson 8

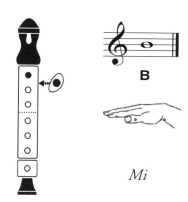

Mi

1. **G** is now the tonal center, *Do*. What note is *Re?*____ *So?*____ *La?*____. Our new note is **B**, *Mi*. (See page iii and pages 62-63 for more on Pentatonic Scales.)

2. **Echo** on **G A B** ; on **G A B D'** ; **E G A B**.

3. Play what you see, following Teacher's hand signs, using only the notes of the **G** pentatonic scale, **D E G A B D' E'**.

4. **Focus** Practice note combinations, silently first: **G B G B** ; **A B B A** ; **G B A B** ; **B D' B D'** ; **D' B D' B** ; **E G B G** ; **D G B G** ; **D G B D'** ; **E' D' E' D'** ; **G B D' E'** ; *etc.*

5. Practice the following scale patterns at different tempi from slow to fast; loud and soft; crescendo and decrescendo; and with various articulation: tongued legato, portato, staccato, and slurred legato.

6. Echo your own phrases in various meters.

7. **Improvise** Make up an Echo Piece, **A A B B** using **E** as the tonal center. Change the form to **A A B B A A**.

8. **Q+A** Practice improvising Q+A phrases. Try by yourself, with a partner, over an AX ostinato on [**G** and **D**], [**E** and **B**], or [**A** and **E**]. Think up other ways too.

9. Work out a dance in *3/4* meter in Rondo form, **A B A C A**, complete with accompaniment and suggested movement. Change the tonal center in **B** and **C**.

My Dancing Top

French Canada

PATTERNS

Frogs Jumping

China

Hard Work for a Grain of Rice

China

Daily Growing

Vermont

The trees they are tall and the leaves they are green.

Man - y a time my true__ love I've seen; Man - y an hour have I

passed all a - lone, My bon - ny lad's a long time a - grow - ing.

Daily Growing from "The Hills of Vermont," Sturgis and Hughes,
G. Schirmer, Inc. 1916

o

1. Echo on **D E G A B D' E'**, using both ♩ ♩ and ♩♩♩ 's.

2. Clap the rhythm of the next song, **Nottamun Town.**

3. Sing it, with this rhythm pattern in **3/2** :
   (How can you change the pattern to fit the **2/2** bar?)

Nottamun Town

Kentucky

1. I rode a gray horse that was called a gray mare,
   With a gray mane and tail, green stripes down her back,
   Gray mane and gray tail, green stripes down her back,
   There wa'nt a hair on her but what was coal black.

2. She stood so still, she threw me to the dirt,
   She tore my hide, and bruised my shirt,
   From saddle to stirrup I mounted again,
   And on my ten toes I rode over the plain.

The Riddle Song

Kentucky

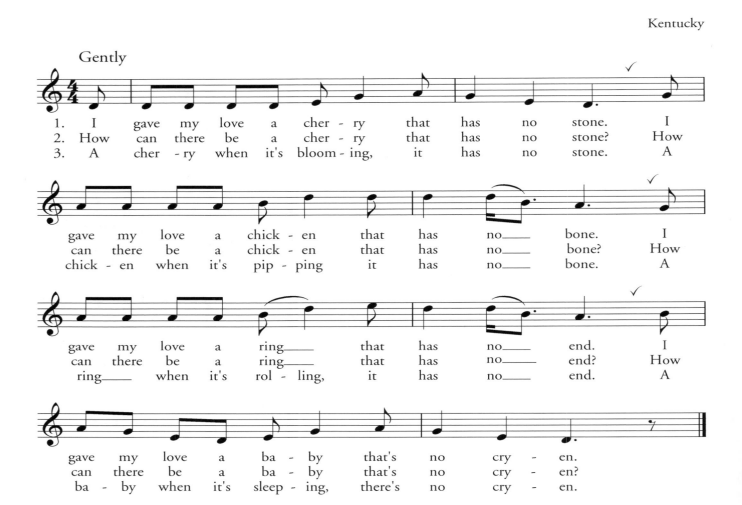

Gently

1. I gave my love a cher - ry that has no stone. I
2. How can there be a cher - ry that has no stone? How
3. A cher - ry when it's bloom - ing, it has no stone. A

gave my love a chick - en that has no___ bone. I
can there be a chick - en that has no___ bone? How
chick - en when it's pip - ping it has no___ bone. A

gave my love a ring___ that has no end. I
can there be a ring___ that has no___ end? How
ring___ when it's rol - ling, it has no___ end. A

gave my love a ba - by that's no cry - en.
can there be a ba - by that's no cry - en?
ba - by when it's sleep - ing, there's no cry - en.

Lesson 9

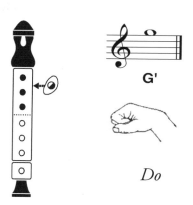

1. High **G′** is fingered just like low **G**, but with the thumb hole partly open. Practice octave skips from **G** to **G′** until your thumb shift is secure.

2. **Focus** Play what you see:

3. Practice at different tempi, with varied articulation.

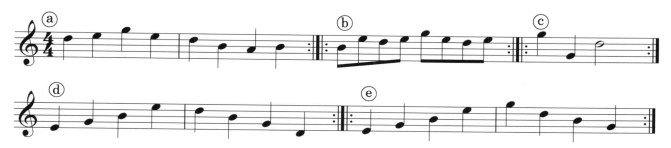

4. **Echo** Take turns being Teacher, echoing on **D′ E′ G′** ; **G B D′ G′** ; **E G A B** ; **D E G A B D′**. Practice by yourself.

5. **Improvise** Make up a longer piece, with three volunteers, each making up a whole section. Decide on the form and the tonal center for each section before you start. Teacher (or a volunteer) makes up an accompaniment pattern to which the soloists must adjust.

6. Again, with new volunteers and new tonal centers. Use three Orff instruments for accompaniment this time, building up from the bottom, "filling the holes" in each previous pattern.

Longing for the Spring Breeze

Taiwan

Fanfare

Isabel Carley

Improvise Hold the drum between your knees, and alternate your hands as you play. Or play on two timps tuned to **G** and **D**. Improvise a march to follow the **Fanfare**, using the **G** pentatonic scale.

The High Mountain

Taiwan

7. Which were the most effective ostinati you made up for these songs? Why?
   Make note of them in the space below, using stick notes and note names, or standard notation.

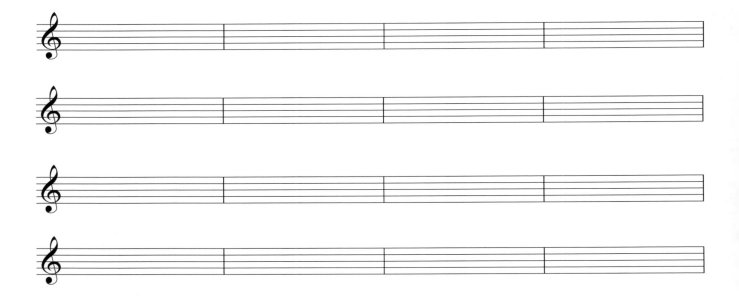

PART III ~ F PENTATONIC

Lesson 10

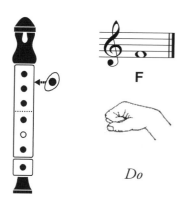

Do

1. **Improvise** Practice moving from low **F** to **C**, silently at first. Which finger moves? Make up an **F - C** ostinato over which Teacher improvises a tune. Again, using SG on the tune. (Remove **E** and **B** bars.)

2. **Echo** Make up echo phrases on **F** and **C** ; **F G A** ; **D F G A**.

3. Follow Teacher's hand signs.
   If **F** is *Do*, what is **G**?_____ **A**?_____ **C**?_____ **D**? _____.

4. Take turns being Teacher, and lead the class with hand signs in Q+A play.

5. Play Q+A using as many notes of the **F** pentatonic scale as you wish.
   Try using *2/4, 3/4, 4/4, 6/8* meters.
   Practice by yourself, using **F**, **D**, and **G** as tonal centers.

6. Play what you see:

7. **Echo** Play exactly the scale patterns Teacher plays, being sure to echo the tonguing.
   Take turns being Teacher.

The Big Drum and the Little Drum

Isabel Carley   Japan

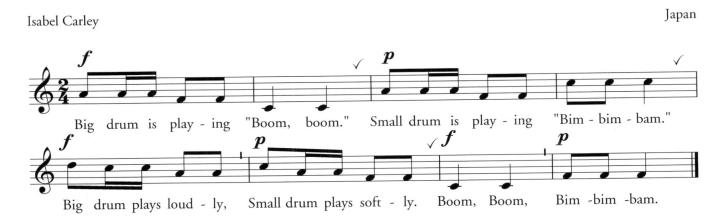

PATTERNS

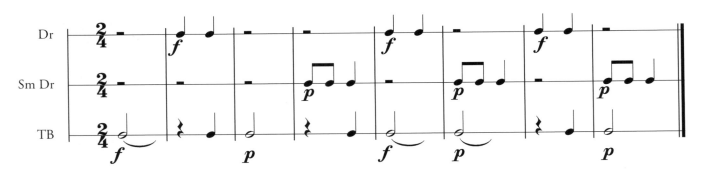

TB = Temple Bell. If you don't have one, you can substitute a Tr (Triangle).

Scottish Croon

Nova Scotia

Quietly and slowly

Pretty Saro

Southern Appalachians

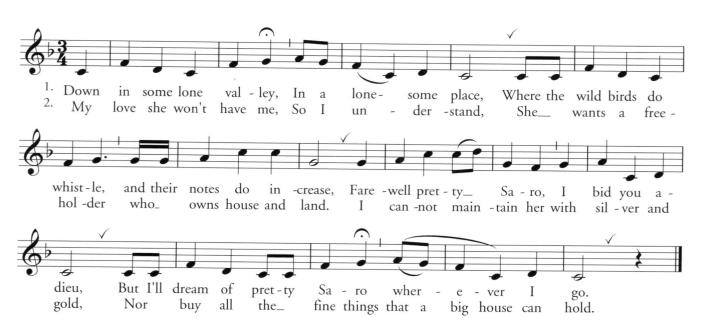

1. Down in some lone val-ley, In a lone-some place, Where the wild birds do
2. My love she won't have me, So I un-der-stand, She__ wants a free-

whist-le, and their notes do in-crease, Fare-well pret-ty__ Sa-ro, I bid you a-
hol-der who__ owns house and land. I can-not main-tain her with sil-ver and

dieu, But I'll dream of pret-ty Sa-ro wher-e-ver I go.
gold, Nor buy all the__ fine things that a big house can hold.

À la Claire Fontaine

French Canada

Andante, very legato

À la clai - re fon - tain - e m'en al - lant pro - men - er,

J'ai trou - vé l'eau si bel - le, que je m'y suis bai - gné,

Lui, y'a long - temps que je t'ai - me, Ja - mais je ne t'ou - blie - rai.

PATTERNS

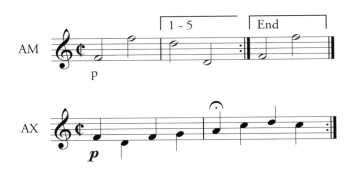

AM

1 - 5   End

AX

Bass on F drone

1. **Echo** Play echo phrases on **C D F G A C′ D′**, with **D** as the tonal center:
    *   all around the class
    *   with a partner
    *   by yourself.

2. **Focus** Sing each of the next three songs with hand signs. (**F** is *Do*.)

Cock Robin

Virginia

2. Who saw him die?
    "It was I," said the fly, "With my little teensy eye."

3. Who made his shroud?
    "It was I," said the beetle, "With my little sewing needle."

4. Who dug his grave?
    "It was I," said the crow, "With my little spade and hoe."

5. Who pat his grave?
    "It was I," said the duck, "With my big old splatter foot."

6. Who preached his funeral?
    "It was I," said the swallow, "Just as loud as I could holler."

Heavy Rain

Taiwan

What is the tonal center? _____

Which two notes would you use for a Drone? ____ and ____.

Canoe Song

Canada

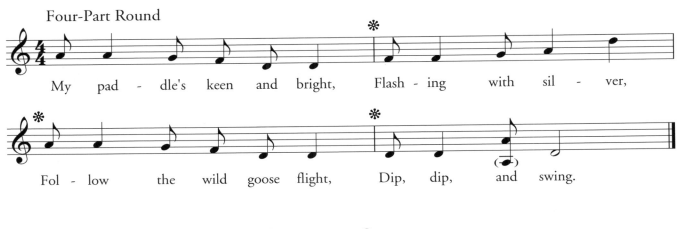

Four-Part Round

My pad - dle's keen and bright, Flash - ing with sil - ver,

Fol - low the wild goose flight, Dip, dip, and swing.

Gtr

If you don't have a guitar, you can adapt the part for AX.

Lesson 11

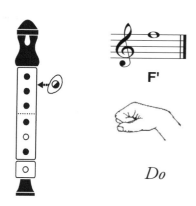

F'

Do

1. What is the difference between the fingerings for high **F'** and low **F**?

2. **Echo** Play what you hear on **F' C'** ; **F' D' C'** ; **F' C' A F** ; **F G A C' D' F'**. Take turns being Teacher. Change the meter or the tonal center when your turn comes.

3. **Improvise** Over Teacher's AX ostinato, improvise all around the class, one phrase each, without interrupting the rhythm. Again, with a new ostinato.

   Focus *Don't double Teacher's rhythm.*
   Your improvisation will be far more interesting if you maintain some rhythmic independence.

4. Play what you see. Practice as needed at different tempi and with varied tonguing.

Harvest Festival

Taiwan

Gaelic Tune

Scotland

Come O'er the Stream, Charlie

Scotland

The Farm Village

Taiwan

Hare Hunting

Isabel Carley   China

Come, come quick- ly, See what I've found here, Tra, la, la! Tra, la, la!

There's a white hare in the bush - es, Tra, la, la! Tra, la, la!

The Red-Cheeked Maiden

Isabel Carley   China

Red - cheeked maiden I love you so,

Red cheeked maiden I love you so,

Since I first saw you long, long a - go,

My own sweet - heart, I still love you so.

Dance

Isabel Carley

SUGGESTED MOVEMENT in Ⓐ Ⓑ Ⓐ FORM:

Ⓐ Circle formation: Bars 1-8   Bars 9-16

Side-step <u>LR</u> L   Same backward to original circle.
                                          <u>LR</u> L stamp at Bars 15-16

Forward R L

Side-step <u>RL</u> R

Forward to center L R   *etc.*

Ⓑ Gallop, hands joined, left to Bar 24; right to Bar 32.

Ⓐ Repeat movement for **Ⓐ**. Or start stepping backward, Bars 1-8; and forward Bars 9-16.

More to Learn

BOOK TWO • RIT Two teaches pentatonic fingering patterns on the alto recorder and expands to the major scales in **F**, **C**, **G**, and **B**♭. The other diatonic modes follow, concluding with shifting chord techniques and paraphony.

Plenty of lovely ideas for student improvisation, and the emphasis on doing first, then, applying literacy is still evident. Students are encouraged to move back and forth between soprano and alto fingerings, at their own pace...[and] are also challenged to build a repertoire of songs, in both fingerings, that they can play by memory. Integration of two or more other Orff media is included in every lesson. ~ Kim Kendrick, *Ostinato*

BOOK THREE • RIT Three is for the advanced student who already plays both **C** and **F** recorders.

The third volume, although specific to recorder, is equally applicable to the musical development of any vocalist or instrumentalist...Carley deftly guides the player through scales, melodic ornamentation, decoration of the third, canons, chord changes, descant creation and free improvisation. She includes many fine musical examples, but the focus is the emphasis on improvisation leading to composition in the forms that parallel the history of Western music. ~ Leslie Timmons, *American Recorder*

About the RIT Book Series

A wonderful series of resource books for teaching recorder in the Orff classroom...Accessible to both experienced and inexperienced teachers...[Carley] is a master teacher. ~ Kim Kendrick

A wealth of practical pedagogy for learning and teaching recorder – a reflection of [Carley's] incomparable musicianship and extensive work with children and adults in ensemble settings... Especially useful for the classroom, but equally appropriate for private instruction, they provide the framework for a curriculum designed to develop comprehensive musicianship. ~ Leslie Timmons

To order, contact your bookseller or visit brasstownpress.com.

Isabel McNeill Carley, Teacher: An Appreciation

As soon as you met her in the classroom, my mother would implicitly set the ground rules. It came through in her manner, her precision of expression, and her concentration on everyone in the room. Please, students, prepare to expend some serious effort. Respond to my dedication and discernment. Come and share my passion for the joy of making original, elegant music. It was a pact. If you would commit to joining her in the pursuit of knowledge and proficiency, she as your teacher would celebrate and reward your efforts and your accomplishments. Her zeal for genuine connection and mutual enrichment kept former students in touch, decades after their shared hours in the classroom.

All these qualities found their way into her writing. Her signature instructional books for the recorder (familiarly, **RIT One**, **Two**, and **Three**) and her essays and published pieces convey that teacher's persona: thoughtful, rigorous, thorough – and sometimes fierce. She just couldn't settle for mediocrity or lifeless musical education. Her three RIT books are gems of pedagogy. Drawn from the wellspring of the Orff approach, their sphinx-like simplicity of presentation may obscure the larger design, at first. But the experienced practitioners soon recognize what's going on, while the less conversant will also find themselves absorbed in this method for playing more freely, with more sensitivity and flair. Persevere, and under my mother's tutelage, you discover for yourself a wonderful creative way to find the music in the air and make it your own.

Take the very first lesson in **RIT One**. It starts with only high C and A on the soprano recorder. These notes lie comfortably one added finger, and a minor third, apart. With only these two notes the student and teacher commence to make music. This is critical. How many approaches to learning music save the good part – actually making music – to some later time? When? Only after countless exercises and drills and games and theory explanations, all punctuated by the (forgettably inane) introductory noteheads on staffs. Not here. Right away, teacher and student are challenged to listen to each other, to share an exploration of song structure, counterpoint, layers of pitched and unpitched percussion ostinati, of songs from various world musical cultures, dance and movement, rhythm and response. Playing the recorder soon begins to feel as if it were as natural as singing or clapping.

For the student, this is an authentic encounter, not a canned, mechanical "lesson." And for anyone teaching from her books, this joint exploration can and should be different each time. You can't phone in these lessons. Imbued with the Orff approach, the classroom experience is so engaging that the pedagogy may pass unnoticed. Yet what a wealth of knowledge and practice habits are being transferred!

An Appreciation (continued)

It's a conceptual knot – how to teach something as original, evanescent, and individual as improvisation. But the knot untangles, imperceptibly, from the first lesson to the last in these three recorder books. Her essays examine and consider in depth the importance of improvisation. In the classroom, though, Isabel Carley's learning program just assumes that everyone can draw on their own creative resources, and in so assuming, makes it possible. I have seen children and adults, with or without previous musical training, respond brilliantly. Their new-found delight in their own capability is contagious.

No beginner is forced to jump into the deep end. Instead, the lessons are gentle increments of development. Echo what Teacher plays, often an improvisation itself. Respond in "Q+A" exchanges, modeling song structure and developing sensitivity to tonal center. Learn new songs, either composed pieces or from world folk traditions. Bridge from what's already known to the unknown – to longer, improvised melodic phrases and more complex compositional forms. Explore the riches of repeated, layered patterns. The learning sequence supports the teacher and makes the progression toward confident playing and improvisation seem unremarkable and easy.

Where does this all lead? Instead of walling off musical resources – dance, instrumental music, singing, percussion, folklore, ensemble playing, music theory, sight-reading – why not take elements from every resource and integrate them into a living, spontaneous experience? I imagine a teacher improvising a class composition that incorporates speech, Brazilian-inspired movement, West African-style body percussion, group singing, and recorder playing. Instead of learning to read music first, you have made music first.

As a student, if after making a new song, you realize you'll want to remember it for later, you gain the skills to notate it. That way, you, and perhaps millions of others, could later recapture that combination of elements that form your new song. Just as my mother was herself a professionally trained musician, there is nothing in her work adverse to the formal aspects of musical education. Yet the emphasis is on retaining the joy of music-making even as conventional knowledge grows. That's the beauty of it.

Ultimately, when I consider my mother's work and legacy, I see sensitive, inspired pedagogy in action. The teacher comes to know that finding the idea for the next "Q+A" melodic exchange will be easy. The student comes to know that spinning out an answer to the next musical question will be fun.

Together, teacher and students confirm to one another that making music doesn't end when the lesson does. There is always something more, waiting to be discovered and played and enjoyed.

Anne M Carley
Charlottesville, Virginia

Body Percussion Patterns

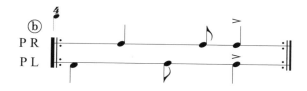

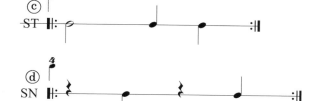

Ostinato Patterns

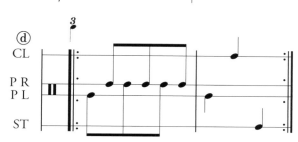

Combinations

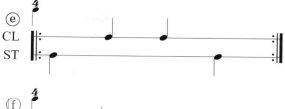

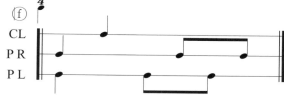

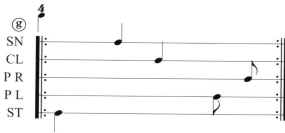

About Pentatonic Scales and Modes

The following tables illustrate the three pentatonic scales and modes that are covered in **RIT One**: **C** (Part I), **G** (Part II), and **F** (Part III). Fingering diagrams for soprano recorder, and solfège note names are also included.

The following characteristics of the pentatonic modes apply generally:

- Only *Do* and *La* Pentatonic modes have complete tonic triads.
- *Re* and *So* Pentatonic have no Third.
- *Mi* Pentatonic has no Fifth.
  Without a Fifth, *Mi* Pentatonic requires a tonic drone, and may, like its diatonic cousin, the Phrygian Mode, use the Fourth or Sixth as the reciting tone.
  It may also make good use of the low Seventh plus or minus a preceding Sixth in cadences.
- *Do* Pentatonic includes both the tonic and submediant (vi) chords.
- *La* Pentatonic includes both the minor tonic and the major mediant (III).
- *Re* Pentatonic melodies require an emphasis on tonic and dominant to be convincing.
  Its scale permits the use of a typically modal VII - i cadence.

SET I C PENTATONIC ~ Scales and Modes

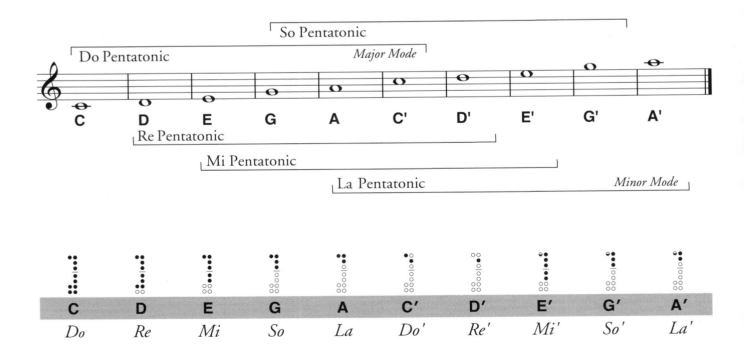

SET II G PENTATONIC ~ Scales and Modes

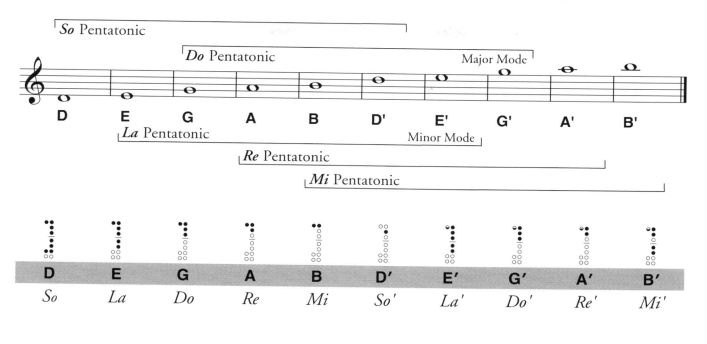

SET III F PENTATONIC ~ Scales and Modes

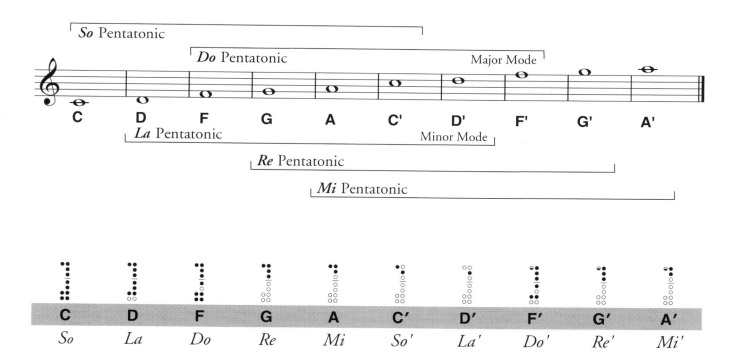

Brasstown Press Editions

Isabel McNeill Carley Orff Essentials Collection

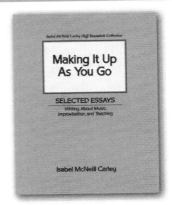

Eleven lessons for beginners and their teachers that explore C, G, and F Pentatonic and related modes on the soprano recorder. 46 songs and introductory exercises.
wire-o ISBN 978-1-931922-46-3
paperback ISBN 978-0-9836545-0-6

Building on RIT One, RIT Two transfers soprano fingering patterns to the alto recorder and introduces hexatonic and diatonic major and minor modes. 52 songs and intermediate exercises.
wire-o ISBN 978-1-931922-07-4
paperback ISBN 978-0-9836545-1-3

For the student already proficient on both C and F recorders. These lessons parallel the material in the Orff Schulwerk (volumes III and V). 46 challenging songs for advanced students.
wire-o ISBN 978-1-93192208-1
paperback ISBN 978-0-9836545-2-0

IM Carley's written work from over thirty years. The essays are grouped in three sections: Origins, Practicum, and Exhortations. Includes biographical sketch and list of IMC's publications.
ISBN 978-0-9836545-3-7

IMC's Five Little Books

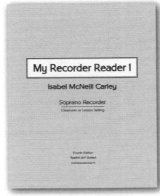

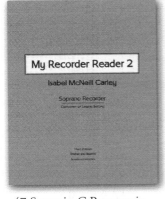

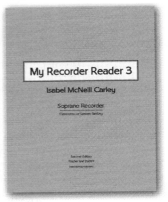

The three **My Recorder Reader** books are a coordinated series of songs to bring a student from elementary playing to a more experienced level. Notes are added one by one to extend the student's range, with minimal instructional comments. The carefully graduated sequence of the pieces facilitates individual mastery and skill development.

41 Songs in G Pentatonic Scale and Modes.
ISBN 978-0-9836545-6-8

47 Songs in C Pentatonic and F Pentatonic.
ISBN 978-0-9836545-7-5

44 Songs. Expanded ranges, Pentatonic to Diatonic.
ISBN 978-0-9836545-8-2

EBOOK!

Establish a secure musical foundation with the step-by-step lessons offered in **My Song Primer** (for singing) and **My Recorder Primer** (for soprano recorder). Songs are interwoven in lessons with speech and rhythm exercises, suggestions for percussion and Orff instruments, and ideas for games and movement.

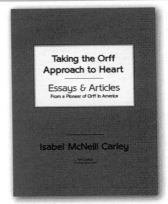

13 Songs, one per lesson, from So-Mi to Pentatonic.
ISBN 978-0-9836545-4-4

35 Songs in 6 Lessons, D-E-G-A range.
ISBN 978-0-9836545-5-1

All new essays and articles plus a read-aloud story.
ISBN 978-0-9836545-9-9

Made in United States
Troutdale, OR
07/18/2023

11392401R00044